FLORA BOTANICA

QUILTS FROM THE SPENCER MUSEUM OF ART

FLORA BOTANICA

QUILTS FROM THE SPENCER MUSEUM OF ART

BY BARBARA BRACKMAN

EDITOR: Deb Rowden
DESIGNER: Kelly Ludwig
ILLUSTRATION: Eric Sears
TECHNICAL EDITOR: Deb McCurnin
PRODUCTION ASSISTANCE: Jo Ann Groves

Photographs of the quilts and other objects from the collection
of the Spencer Museum of Art are by Robert Hickerson.
Floral photographs are by Barbara Brackman.
Several of the period lithographs and prints are from
the collection of the Library of Congress.

PUBLISHED BY: Kansas City Star Books
1729 Grand Blvd.
Kansas City, Missouri, USA 64108

First edition, first printing
ISBN: 978-1-935362-04-3
Library of Congress Control Number: 2008942701
Printed in the United States of America by Walsworth Publishing Co., Marceline, MO

To order copies, call StarInfo at (816) 234-4636 and say "Books."

PickleDish.com
The Quilter's Home Page

www.PickleDish.com

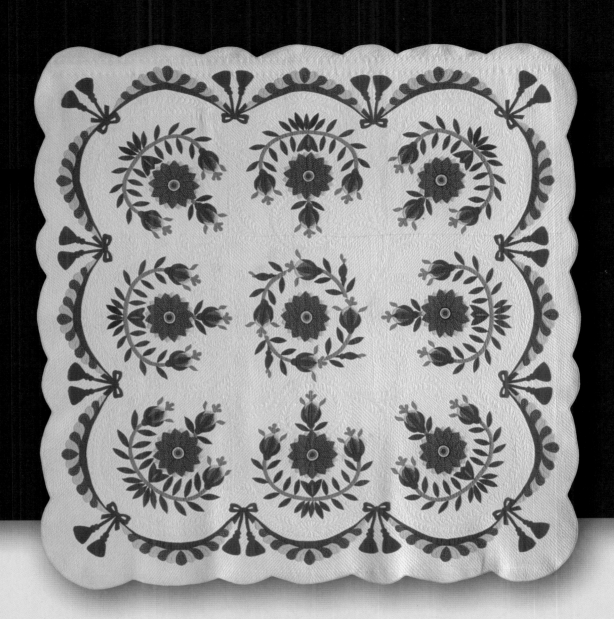

CONTENTS

FLORA BOTANICA

AN EXHIBITION AT THE SPENCER MUSEUM OF ART
JULY 5—OCTOBER 26, 2008

>>> Richard Klocke and the Exhibits Design Department painted quilt blocks on the grass for the show opening in June, 2008

<<< **Christina Hays Malcom**
circa 1820-before 1884, United States
Sunflower quilt, circa 1840-1884
cotton, appliqué, quilting
Gift of Miss Iva James, 1972.0125
80 1/2" x 75 1/2"

Christina Malcom made this quilt for her son Jonathan, stitching his name on the back. Though she was born in North Carolina, Christina spent much of her life in Indiana, a state whose sunflowers seem to have inspired her unusual quilt. Floral designs provide inspiration for many quilts, yet few quilters actually drew from nature. This quilt seems to be an exception. She carefully observed the broad, almost heart-shaped leaves, the sturdy stalk, and the golden petals.

<<<**Julia A. Chalmers Smith**
circa 1825-?, United States, New York
Sunburst quilt, circa 1840-1880
cotton, piecing, quilting
William Bridges Thayer Memorial, 1928.0915
93" x 94"

According to a label relating family history, Julia Chalmers made this quilt before her marriage in Galway, New York. The complex pieced design was named Sun, Sunburst, or Rising Sun in twentieth-century quilt pattern literature. We can also view it as a sunflower, an abstraction of nature's geometry.

Botanical images have been among the most popular in United States quilts. Rather than drawing directly from their gardens, most quiltmakers drew from centuries of folk art traditions. The abstractions we see as fruits and flowers can be traced to many cultures on many continents, including Greek mythology, the Judeo-Christian Bible, and Islamic, Indian, and Persian traditions. This exhibition examines sources and symbolism in floral pattern from various perspectives. Quilts range in age from the late-18th century to the recent past, including several new quilts drawn from the old patterns in the Spencer collection.

The Helen Foresman Spencer Museum of Art at The University of Kansas, considered one of the nation's finest university art museums, maintains a collection of more than 25,000 art objects. The university art collection was established in 1917 when Kansas City art collector Sallie Casey Thayer (1856-1925) loaned nearly 7,500 art objects to the University of Kansas to form a museum "to encourage the study of fine arts in the Middle West." The University of Kansas Museum of Art was formally established in 1928 in Spooner Hall. Mrs. Thayer then gave her collection to the museum as the William Bridges Thayer Memorial Collection. The current building was built through a 1974 gift of $4.6 million from Helen Foresman Spencer, a Kansas City collector and patron of the arts. The neo-classical building, built of Indiana limestone, was designed by Kansas City architect Richard Jenks and had its grand opening in January, 1978.

The Spencer Museum of Art has an impressive collection of about 180 quilts with origins in the gift from Sallie Casey Thayer. Soon after her marriage to William Thayer, owner of the Emery, Bird, Thayer department store, she began her collecting passion with a single blue and white tile from a home slated to be demolished. Collecting and showing her artwork became her life work. She acquired objects eclectically. Her interests included Japanese prints, European glass

and American silver. She had the foresight to gather many types of art, including American textiles, before museums perceived their value.

Fifty-three quilts were included in the 7,500 objects she donated to the University. Sallie Casey Thayer chose her quilts well. A few are rare eighteenth-century examples and many are early nineteenth-century designs pieced of exceptional cotton prints.

The Thayer quilts were first displayed in a 1920 textile exhibit in the halls of the administration building at the university. The collection attracted the interest of quilt lovers like Rose Kretsinger and Carrie Hall, who included a few Thayer quilts in their 1935 book, *The Romance of the Patchwork Quilt in America*. Hall donated her impressive collection of 800 quilt blocks and patterns to the University in the 1930s and in 1971, Mary Kretsinger donated quilts made by her mother, Rose, and her grandmother, Anna Gleissner Good. The following year Iva James of Hutchinson, Kansas gave the museum 18 quilts made by women in the James and Malcom families. The collection has increased over the years, with gifts from generous donors of a single quilt or a small group of three or four. The quilts are kept in climate controlled storage, with most rolled around acid-free cardboard cylinders and covered with dust protectors of cotton sheeting to protect them for future generations.

Members of the Kaw Valley Quilters' Guild stitched reproductions of Spencer quilts. This catalog includes patterns for five copies of quilts inspired by tradition. These quilts were loaned by the quilt artists, who also gave us permission to include patterns for their designs.

The exhibit was organized by Barbara Brackman, the Spencer's honorary curator of quilts. The quilt collection at the Spooner-Thayer Museum inspired her interest in antique quilts when she was a KU student in the 1960s. Carrie Hall's collection of blocks and patterns motivated her to index quilt patterns in her own encyclopedias of pieced and appliquéd designs and she has featured many of the Spencer's quilts in her books. Among her recent books for Kansas City Star Books are *Carrie Hall's Sampler* and *Borderland in Butternut and Blue*.

THE EXHIBIT

The 27 quilts pictured on the pages that follow were included in an exhibit titled Quilts: *Flora Botanica*, on view at the Spencer Museum of Art at the University of Kansas, July 12-October 12, 2008. The exhibit examined sources and symbolism in floral pattern from various perspectives. These quilts range in age from the late-18th century to the recent past, including several new quilts drawn from the old patterns in the Spencer collection.

Susan Stayman won awards at the 1866 Kansas State Fair for "two fancy patch quilts, of entirely original design." This splendid quilt may have been one of them. Family stories say it also won a prize at an Illinois fair in 1855. Her daughter called it Moss Rose, which to Victorian gardeners meant a variety of hybrid rose with a sticky, aromatic "moss" on the stems and leaves.

Roses were quiltmakers' favorite floral images. Few are as detailed as this representation with thorns and naturalistic buds. The border features a simpler wild rose, a five-petaled flower. Stayman may have drawn roses directly from her garden, but four similar quilts have been found in Iowa, Michigan, Pennsylvania and Washington. A truly "original" floral design is rare in nineteenth-century quilts.

Quilters can appreciate Stayman's masterful handwork. She used a blanket stitch (also called a buttonhole stitch) to cover the patches' raw edges. It is unfortunate she chose the solid pink fabric for her wild rose border because it's lost much color over the years. The green and Turkey-red cottons were more reliable.

<<< **Susan Black Stayman**
1828-?, United States, Illinois
Moss Rose quilt, 1853
cotton, appliqué, quilting
Gift of Miss Mary Stayman, 1949.0024.01
72" x 73"

"The Moss Rose," lithograph published by N. Currier, circa 1847. Collection of the Library of Congress

This appliquéd quilt must be the other of the pair of "fancy patch quilts of entirely original design" that won acclaim at the 1866 Kansas State Fair. The needlework is certainly exceptional with quilting measuring 12 stitches to an inch (measured on the top of the quilt). Quilters are usually content with eight or nine stitches per inch.

Stayman looked to folk art traditions where this flat, eight-lobed shape has long represented the rose, a powerful cultural symbol. The name Dahlia Wreath is from the family. Other published names are Wreath of Roses and Kentucky Rose.

Stayman's concept of original design probably differed from ours. Hundreds of similar quilts survive. Within folk art's strict boundaries she created small innovations, for example, the specific arrangement of 32 leaves on each wreath and the border geometry, a clever pattern of modular arcs forming a running vine.

›› **Susan Black Stayman**
1828-?, United States, Illinois
Dahlia Wreath quilt, 1855
cotton, appliqué, quilting
Gift of Miss Mary Stayman, 1949.0025.02
88" x 89"

*A*bout 1930, Minnie Moodie, first curator at the University of Kansas's art museum, donated this quilt to the Thayer Museum, as it was then known. She called it Rose of Sharon, a metaphor from the King James Version of the Bible.

"I am the rose of Sharon, and the lily of the valleys." (Solomon 2:1)

The pattern relies on several design conventions typical of Germanic folk arts. Cookie-cutter shaped roses bloom in triplicate, growing from a vase here abstracted to a tiny triangle. The smaller flowers viewed in profile might be buds, but are often seen as lilies or tulips.

The red and green palette was a standard color scheme for quilts, also popular in German traditional arts. Quilters were willing to pay extra for Turkey-red cotton because it did not bleed or fade. However, the colorfast dye was hard on the fibers. Use and washing over the years can cause it to shred.

<<< **Rena Coon Thomas**
United States, Illinois
Rose of Sharon quilt, circa 1870-1890
cotton, appliqué, quilting
Gift of Mrs. Minnie S. Moodie, 0000.0037
89" x 67"

The unknown quiltmaker exercised a good deal of creativity within the constraints of traditional folk art. Stylized florals sprout from a footed urn in the typical red and green color scheme. Drooping tulips neatly fill the square block format.

Sallie Casey Thayer, whose eclectic collection was the original basis for the Spencer Museum's archives, donated dozens of quilts to the University of Kansas around 1915. This well-worn piece from the Thayer donation provided inspiration for Doris Lux's new interpretation.

<<< Doris Lux
Meriden, Kansas
cotton, appliqué, quilting
Flower Pot, 2007
38 1/2" x 38 1/2"
For a pattern of this miniature version, see page 66.

>>> Artist Unknown
United States
Flower Pot quilt, circa 1840-1870
cotton, appliqué, quilting
William Bridges Thayer Memorial,
1928.0907
72" x 72"

Artist Unknown
United States
plate, 1867
earthenware, slip
William Bridges Thayer Memorial,
1928.3084
A Pennsylvania-German artist decorated a
redware plate with a stylized floral during
the period when red and green floral quilts
were popular.

his lively quilt features a geometric pieced design bordered with an appliquéd floral vine on just **two sides.** Today's quiltmakers speculate that seamstresses making such quilts planned to cover a bed pushed up to the bedroom wall, saving time and stitches by sewing only what would be displayed. Today's aesthetics frame quilts as art on the wall, so Gail Stewart's recent interpretation features a symmetrical border.

The border's floral images, possibly roses and tulips, can be traced to many ancient cultures—Islamic, Indian and European. The border tulip seen in profile is abstracted further into geometric shapes in the blocks. Similar patterns are called Sagebud or Lily Pond. Others see bird footprints in the block, and use names like Goose Tracks and Duck Paddle.

<<< Artist Unknown
United States
Sagebud or Goose Tracks Variation quilt,
circa 1840-1875
cotton, piecing, appliqué, quilting
William Bridges Thayer Memorial,
1928.0936
80" x 69"

>>> Gail Stewart
Overland Park, Kansas
Goose Tracks, 2007
cotton, piecing, appliqué, quilting
40" x 40"
For a pattern of this miniature version, see page 77.

$\mathcal{T}$he unknown maker, grandmother of the donor, used the favorite fabrics of the mid-nineteenth century quiltmaker to create a geometric design echoing the stylized triple florals of traditional Germanic ornament and earlier Persian and Indian imagery.

Her block is known in today's quilt lexicon as North Carolina Lily, a name that really doesn't reflect where the quilts were made. In 1929 Ruth Finley published a romantic if dubious story that cast the name in print: The "lily in its migration from coast to coast acquired eight different names, evidently bestowed in honor of the wild lilies native to each region....It was called 'The North Carolina Lily', all through the South except in Kentucky and Tennessee where it was known as 'The Mountain Lily....'" Finley's inspiration was a wildflower native to the southeastern woodlands. The Carolina Lily (*lilium michauxii*) is a small spotted flower similar to what midwesterners call tiger lilies.

>>> **Grandmother of Willis C. McEntarfer**
United States
North Carolina Lily quilt, circa 1840-1860
cotton, piecing, appliqué, quilting
Gift of Willis C. McEntarfer, Hoyt, Kansas,
1973.0120
85" x 85 1/2"

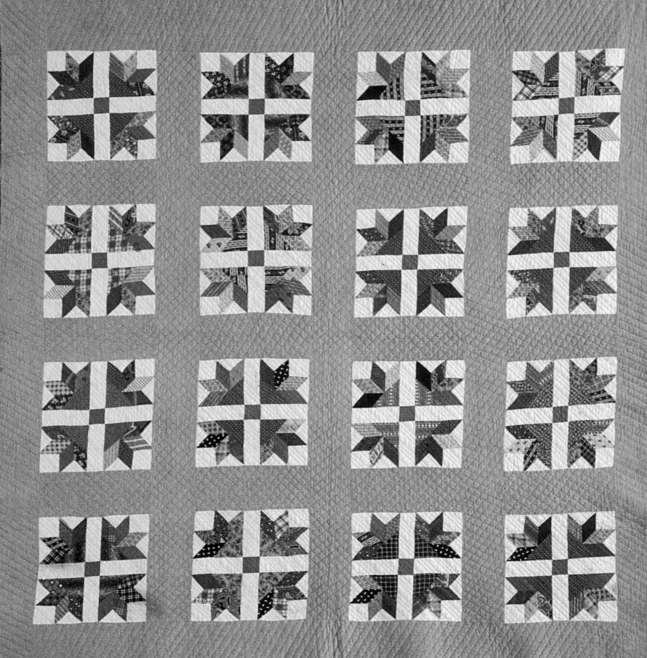

$\mathcal{A}$ccording to the family history Christina Malcom finished this quilt in Indiana before her death in 1884. Her pieced quilts appear to have been made in a short span of time using a scrap bag of prints fashionable in the 1870s and 1880s. This quilt shows off some of the era's popular prints, calicos in madder shades from plum to chocolate and brick red. Periwinkle blue calicos were quite up-to-date at the time and offer a good clue to the 1880 period. Christina punctuated her scrap quilt with spots of green calico and framed the blocks with a wide sashing of double-pink calico.

The pattern, a version of the classic tulip or lily, has many recorded names, most inspired by the garden: Lily Pond, Sage Bud and Fancy Flowers; and some by birds seen through the kitchen window: Duck Paddle, Goose Tracks, Crow's Foot and Dove in the Window

<<< Christina Hays Malcom
circa 1820-before 1884, United States
Goose Tracks quilt, circa 1840-1884
cotton, piecing, quilting
Gift of Miss Iva James, 1972.0127
80" x 73"

>>> Jerrye Van Leer
Lawrence, Kansas
Dove in the Window, 2006
28" x 28"
For a pattern of this miniature version, see
page 84.

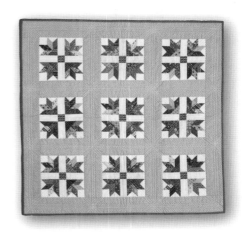

*H*ere we have a faded beauty, a once impressive masterpiece by an unknown maker who used a floral vine border to frame pieced blocks in a design published as Star and Crescent or Star of the West. Details include a corded insert (piping) in the binding and around the patchwork center, indicating a date of 1840 to 1865, when similar piping was a popular feature in women's dresses, still stitched by hand.

American quilters loved Turkey red for their quilts. The imported fabric did not bleed from washing or fade from light, but abrasion easily wore the surface. This quilt must have been used and washed often, resulting in much fabric loss. Mid-century greens do not often fade, but a well-meaning owner may have bleached the quilt.

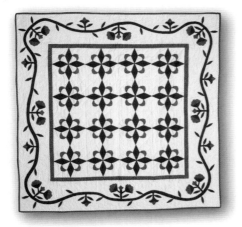

‹‹‹ Julie McEathron
Lawrence, Kansas
Star and Crescent, 2007
cotton, piecing, appliqué, quilting
50" x 50"
For a pattern of this reproduction, see page 72.

››› Artist Unknown
United States
Star and Crescent quilt, circa 1840-1865
cotton, piecing, appliqué, quilting
William Bridges Thayer Memorial,
1928.0904
75" x 75"

This four-block quilt by an unknown maker shows real skill in the appliqué stitches and unusual design. The blocks were probably made between 1840 and 1880 and set together, bordered and quilted at a later date. Quilting stitches and quilting design (a one-inch grid) reflect lower standards for needlework typical at the end of the century.

The pattern is often viewed as a bud or a tulip, but its basic identity relates to the pomegranate used for centuries in Asian and European decorative arts. The fruit is split in profile, often depicted with remnants of the blossom on top and the leaves below.

Pomegranates have rich symbolism in many cultures. In Jewish metaphor the fruit is considered to have 613 seeds—corresponding to the Torah's 613 commandments. The Muslim Koran mentions it as a gift from Allah. Christian symbolism suggests it as the forbidden fruit in the Garden of Eden (a possible reason for the quilt pattern name Love Apple). It was also a forbidden fruit in Greek myth where Persephone brought about winter's curse by eating its seeds.

English embroiderers borrowing fanciful images from India, China, and the Muslim world decorated textiles with pomegranates in their Jacobean-style crewel work. Spanish conquistadors brought the image of *la granada* to New Spain where we still see it in the Navajo squash blossom.

<<< Artist Unknown
United States
Four Block Tulip quilt, 1840-1900
cotton, appliqué, quilting
Gift of Edith Benson, Lawrence, 1970.0206
73 1/2" x 66 1/2"

Florals have long been the most popular imagery in printed cottons. The two block-printed fabrics in this early quilt were fashionable for clothing and furnishings. Naturalistic sprays and bouquets are arranged in a style fabric historians call "floral trails," an arrangement imitating nature. The blossoms, however, are rather fanciful abstractions that may represent tulips, roses and carnations, Western ornament's standard blooms.

When Sallie Casey Thayer donated this quilt, one of the oldest in her collection, she indicated that it·had belonged to the family of founding father Alexander Hamilton. It is definitely old enough to have graced a bed in his home (Hamilton died after a duel with Aaron Burr in 1804) but there is no other evidence of that association.

>>> **Artist Unknown**
United States
Check quilt, circa 1790-1825
cotton, piecing, quilting
William Bridges Thayer Memorial, 1928.0914
90 1/2" x 75" (without the fringe)

The unknown quiltmaker embroidered her initials "M.A.C." on the reverse of this quilt that reflects changes in printing technology. About 1800 fabric manufacturers invented faster methods with one important innovation being the roller or cylinder printing press. Roller prints gave seamstresses more variety at lower costs. Fabric designers created pattern with small repeats suitable for the roller and generated new ideas for the mass market. Floral designs were plotted into regularly spaced grids that designers call "foulards." Geometrics, particularly printed plaids, became popular.

<<< "M.A.C."
United States
Four Patch quilt, circa 1820-1840
cotton, piecing, quilting, embroidered
initials
William Bridges Thayer Memorial,
1928.0934
107" x 97"

The earliest published quilt pattern yet found in America shows how to make this design, called Hexagon, Six-sided and Honey-comb patchwork in an 1831 girls' magazine. Another early name was recorded in an 1856 novel describing "Job's troubles, that is to say, innumerable bits of red, yellow and varicolored calico, cut in hexagonal form…" In the 1930s the pattern was revived as Grandmother's Flower Garden.

The unknown quiltmaker used an indigo blue calico to create consistent "paths" in her garden. For the border she cut a green furnishing print into strips. The chintz features flowers arranged in striped sets between architectural columns hung with bouquets. These "pillar prints" reflect American fascination with classical design in the early nineteenth century.

>>> **Artist Unknown**
United States
Hexagon quilt, circa 1825-1850
cotton, piecing, quilting
William Bridges Thayer Memorial,
1928.0926
101" x 96"

Industrialization in the fabric mills eventually caused a design standardization reflected in the calicoes here, simple prints only suggesting florals. Catherine Landis seems to have been more interested in creating effects in color and patchwork than in showing off a variety of fabrics. Her bold coloring makes it difficult to analyze the patchwork pattern, a simple pinwheel block of dark and light triangles paced on point. It's also difficult to date this quilt as the calicos were standards over a long period of time. It may be that the blocks were made in the middle of the nineteenth century and the quilt finished at the end.

Her relatives, sisters Maude and May Landis, donated this quilt and much more to the University of Kansas. Their names live on through scholarships in nursing and mathematics.

<<< Catherine Grabill Landis
United States
Windmill quilt, circa 1880-1910
cotton, piecing, quilting
Gift of Misses Maude and May Landis,
1949.0016.01
89" x 93"

A 17th century English stump work picture of a feast. Three-dimensional stump work is rarely seen in quilts. The photograph is from The History of English Secular Embroidery by M. Jourdain (New York: E.P. Dutton, 1912) page 64.

Olive Batchelor Wells created a unique masterpiece telling the Biblical tale of Adam and Eve's expulsion from paradise. Among the embroidered inscriptions is a hand pointing to the title "The Garden of Eden." She labeled the three-dimensional central flower "Plant of Renown," a reference to a line from the Biblical Book of Ezekiel: "And I will raise up for them a plant of renown, and they shall be no more consumed with hunger in the land..."

The flower might be viewed as a promise of an abundant harvest, but Wells likely saw symbolism described in this early-nineteenth-century sermon:

"Christ gets a great many metaphorical names and descriptions in scripture; sometimes he is called a Rose, sometimes he is called a Sun, and sometimes he is called a Door, sometimes he is called the Tree of life...here he is called a Plant, and a renowned Plant..."

The Plant of Renown and the rose image offer the Old Testament hope of a future Redeemer.

Wells used a variety of needlework techniques. Particularly unusual are Adam and Eve in an old-fashioned embroidery style called stump work in which three-dimensional figures are attached to the surface. Many of her flowers were gathered in another three-dimensional technique called ruching.

Extraordinary as this piece is, quilt historians found one similar in an Ohio museum. A neighbor in Painesville, Ohio, used the same lettering, fabrics and techniques to create a patriotic quilt. Both were shown at the 1856 Lake County Fair, attracting notice from the local newspaper. "There was among numerous other beautiful ones, a Worked Quilt representing the Garden of Eden, in which were Adam and Eve, the tree of forbidden fruit, and, and, which attracted much attention."

>>> **Olive Batchelor Wells**
1822-1893, United States, Ohio
Garden of Eden quilt, 1840-1856
cotton, wool, linen, appliqué, embroidered,
beaded, stump work, quilting
Gift of Mr. and Mrs. C. Wells Haren,
1978.0071
86" x 76"

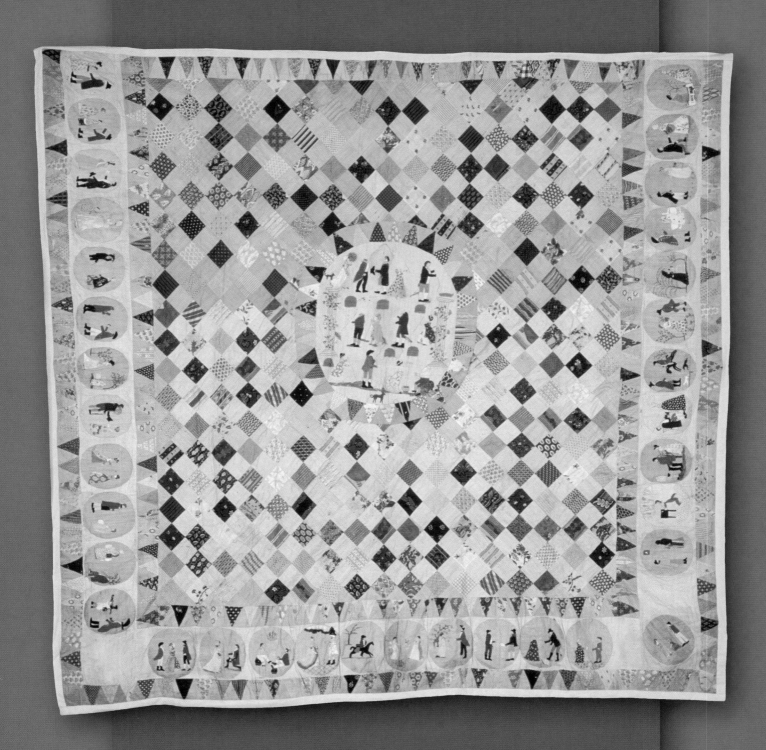

This early English quilt is quite unusual in its depictions of small scenes from everyday life. Each character in the center and border is portrayed in a type of three-dimensional stump work known as a "dressed picture," figures cut from paper and clad in fabric. Over the past two hundred years the paper bodies and silk faces have deteriorated, but embroidered and tucked details of their costume remain. Note the wool uniforms of the "redcoat" soldiers fighting in the Napoleonic wars.

The central panel appears to be a grassy commons or churchyard with festively dressed figures raking mounds of hay or grass. The yard is framed by a pair of classical columns hung with floral vines, much like the pillar prints of the era.

Quilt historian Nancy Hornback writes: "Some of the scenes, viewed in sequence, seem to tell a story: a woman and a man meet; he proposes; he goes off on a ship; they marry, she gets news of peace; he rides home; she presents him with twins." She has identified several possible makers in the donor's family of vicars, farmers, and military men who lived in Yorkshire in England's north.

The patchwork coverlet, like many early English quilts, was never meant to be quilted. Before the piece came to the Spencer collection the donor's aunt, worried about deteriorating fabrics, attached a bedsheet backing and brought the edges over the front for support.

<<< Artist Unknown
England
Pictorial quilt, circa 1790-1810
cotton, linen, silk, wool, raffia, paper,
piecing, appliqué, stump work, embroidery,
ink
Gift of Mr. and Mrs. Harold D. Hedges
in memory of Mr. and Mrs. R. Lockard,
1980.0019
100" x 100"

The Princess Feather with its radiating arms was one of the most popular nineteenth-century appliqué designs. Spencer's collection contains several examples including one dated 1818, an early use of the image.

Quilt pattern copywriters have linked the design to the heraldic badge of the Prince of Wales in which three ostrich plumes represent the heir to the British throne. The future King Edward VII made a popular tour of the United States in the 1850s as Prince of Wales when this quilt top was likely made. It may be that Mary Ann Elliot's inspiration was the romance of British royalty, but a more homely reference—and one just as familiar to nineteenth century gardeners—was an American plant commonly called Prince's Feather. *Amaranthus hypochondriacus*, which has showy red and green leaves like our Christmas poinsettia, looks very much like this windblown design. Author Willa Cather referred to the colorful wildflower in *O Pioneers*, describing "the wind...teasing the prince's feather by the door."

>>> **Mary Ann Seeling Kile Elliot**
United States, 1831-1915
Princess Feather quilt, circa 1840-1950
cotton, appliqué, quilting
Gift of Barbara Kile Zernickow, 1986.0243
97 1/2" x 90"

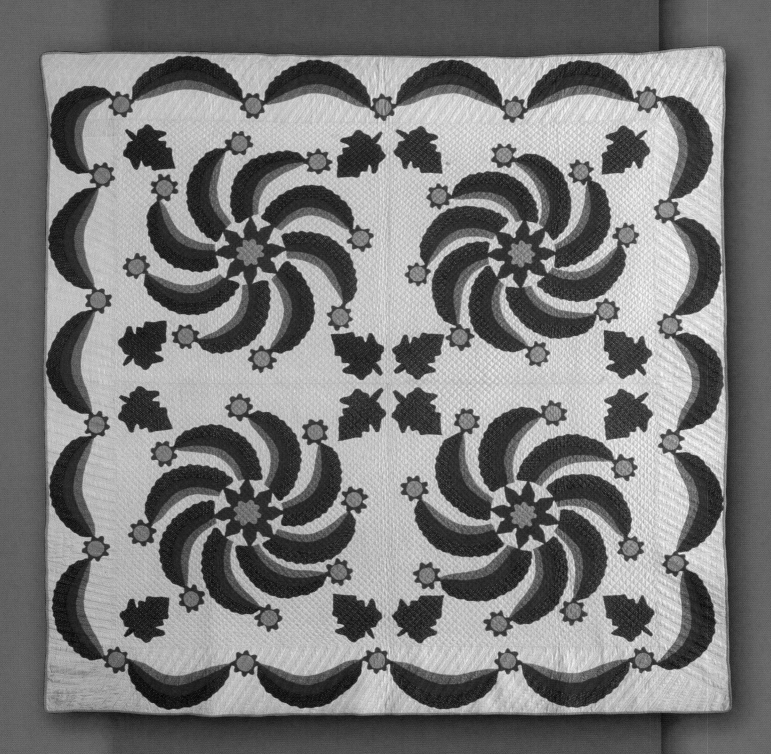

Christina Malcom quilted her son Jonathan's name and the date 1873 into this quilt, one of two she made for him. We know little about her. Jonathan and his father William came to Kansas in 1884 after their wives had died in Indiana, bringing about 25 of Christina's quilts. The Spencer has thirteen, donated by his niece.

This variation of the popular Princess Feather design features florals hanging rather precariously from the whirling feathers. Naturalistic leaves lie in the corners of each of the four blocks. Several similar quilts survive in Kentucky and Indiana. Can this be a regional pattern handed from quilter to quilter?

<<< Christina Hays Malcom
United States, Indiana, circa 1820-before 1884
Princess Feather quilt, 1873
cotton, appliqué, quilting
Gift of Miss Iva James, 1972.0123
85" x 85"

⋙ Margaret Cane
United States, Ohio
Sugar Bowl or Basket quilt, circa 1850-1867
cotton, piecing, appliqué, quilting
Gift of Mrs. L. E. McPherson 1980.0038
83" x 83"

$\mathcal{T}$his quilt has a note stitched to the back indicating that the top was brought from Delaware County, Ohio, to Lawrence, Kansas in 1867 and quilted there. The pieced baskets, popular after 1850, are placed so there is no top or bottom, a view more suited to a bed than a wall.

The quilt owes much of its primitive charm to the spindly vine border. The leggy climber reaching for light seems drawn from the natural world rather than from any lush, imaginary garden.

⋘ Gloria Donohue
Olathe, Kansas
Sugar Bowl or Basket, 2007
cotton, piecing, appliqué, quilting
24 1/2" x 24 1/2"

Gloria Donohue captured the naïve quality of the original in updated fabrics. For a pattern of this reproduction, see page 88.

This quilt, stained and yellowed from hard laundering and poor storage, is an important record of pattern and sewing skills that were almost forgotten by the end of the nineteenth century. The roses are a combination of piecing and appliqué . The border vine at first glance appears to be appliquéd, but closer examination reveals it to be inset, a difficult feat of needlework.

The floral image circled by smaller motifs is often called Whig Rose. In 1911, a magazine writer claimed, "The Whig Rose and the Democrat Rose...were planned for political quilts. They came into existence during the Harrison-Tyler campaign [of 1840]." The name Whig comes to us from England. Although today we hear a ring of pomposity, Whigs viewed themselves as populists supporting a strong Congress in the face of autocratic Presidents, particularly Democrat Andrew Jackson.

<<< **Martha Biggers Burn**
United States
Rose and Bud quilt, circa 1840-1870
cotton, piecing, appliqué, quilting
William Bridges Thayer Memorial,
1928.0906
91 1/2" x 72"

"Ornithology," a political cartoon by Edward Williams Clay in 1852 portrays Whig Presidential candidate Winfield Scott as a turkey and Democrat Franklin Pierce as a rooster. Collection of the Library of Congress.

*H*ow does a Whig Rose differ from a Democrat Rose? Today's quilt writers apply the names interchangeably to nineteenth-century rose patterns, but quilt historian Florence Peto, writing in the 1940s, discussed the differences. A Democrat Rose had cockscombs around the central flower. She speculated that the comb shape represented the Democratic rooster. We're familiar with the Democratic donkey, but the rooster was the image party's symbol in the mid-nineteenth century. A Whig Rose then would be a rose without the combs. One occasionally comes across a quilt embellished with the Whig symbol—a raccoon.

This quilt top was made in Ohio by a member of the Gunckel family (also spelled Kunkel) who moved in 1885 to the German-American community in Eudora, Kansas. The corner blocks are a different green today because the maker used two differently dyed cottons. The corner greens were probably colored with natural dyes, blue overdyed with yellow. The others were probably dyed with a synthetic green, a new dye that became available about 1875. Cottons dyed with early synthetic dyes have a tendency to fade to a khaki shade.

>>> **Elizabeth Gunckel**
died 1888, United States, Ohio
California Rose or Democrat Rose quilt top,
circa 1870-1887
cotton, appliqué
Gift of Elizabeth A. Hazlett in memory of
Emma Kunkel, 1982.0062
67" x 66 1/2"

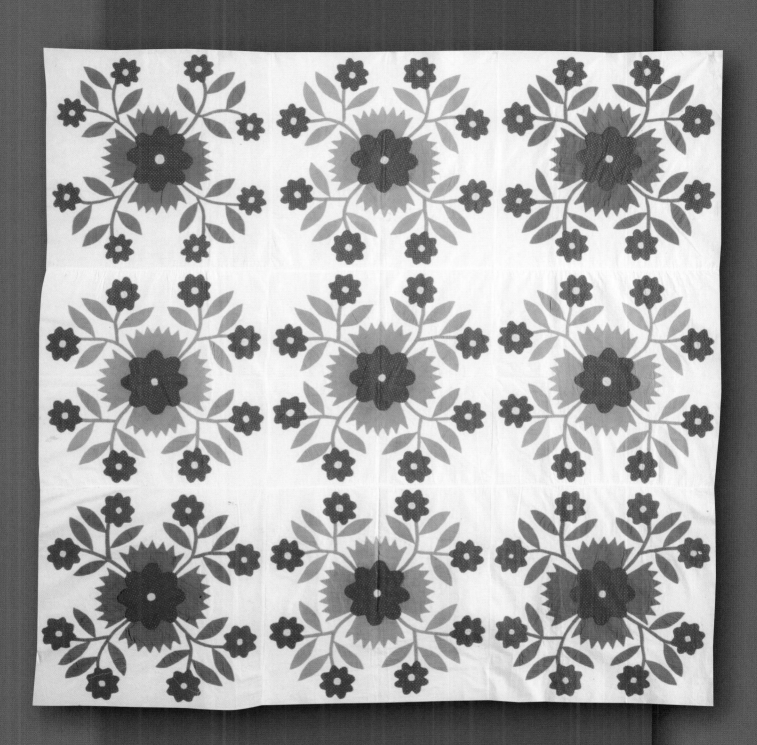

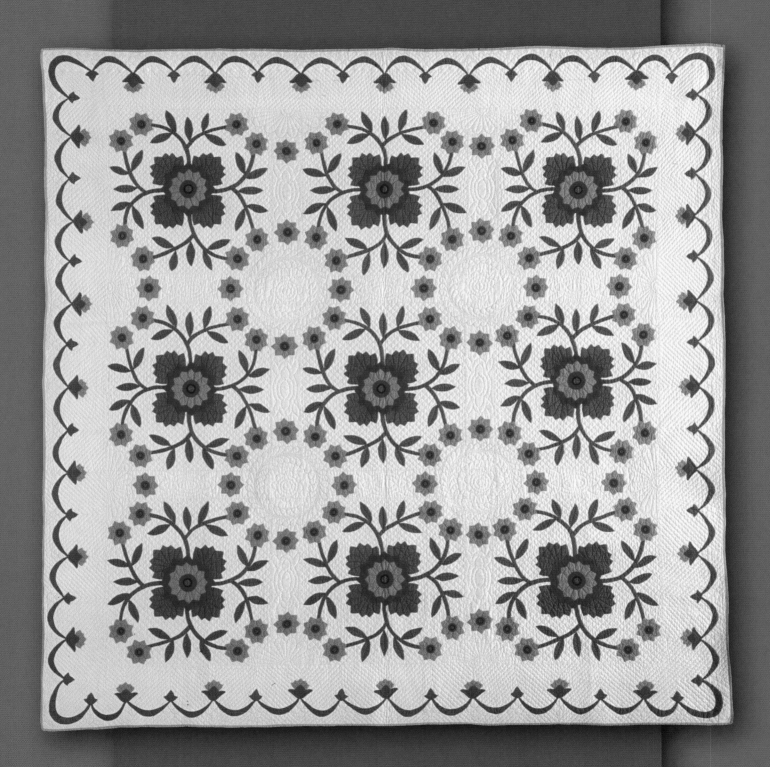

ose Kretsinger was a professional designer with a degree from the School of the Art Institute of Chicago where she took classes from Alphonse Mucha and other leaders in the Arts and Crafts movement. She began making quilts inspired by antiques during the 1920s. This piece was drawn from a damaged quilt belonging to the hired girl who worked in the Kretsinger's Emporia home.

Contrasting it to Elizabeth Gunckel's version of the same design made 50 years earlier, we can see Rose's skills in making subtle changes to folk designs. By extending the stems and standardizing the flower placement, she has created a secondary wreath-like pattern that vies for the viewer's attention.

Her handwritten notes refer to this quilt as Democrat Rose. In bipartisan spirit she and Carrie Hall called it Antique Rose in their 1935 book *The Romance of the Patchwork Quilt in America*.

<<< Rose Frances Good Kretsinger
United States, Kansas, 1886-1963
Democrat Rose quilt, 1926
cotton, appliqué, quilting
Gift of Mary Kretsinger, Emporia, Kansas,
1971.0092
87" x 89"

>>> Artist Unknown
United States
Crazy Quilt, circa 1880-1900
silk, cotton, pieced, appliqué, embroidered, painted
Gift of Dr. E. M. Owens, 1940.0004
73" x 72"

Quilters working after 1880 grew weary of conventionalized florals in red and green as changes in technology and taste created new needlework fads. Commercial patterns replaced folk art traditions and hand-to-hand pattern sharing. Inexpensive silks and renewed interest in embroidery inspired needlewomen to lavish time on the purely decorative Crazy Quilt.

Floral vignettes in paint and stitches reflect a new fascination with Japanese design in the cat tails and fans. We see traces of European arts and crafts principles in the sunflower image and the naturalistic golden rod. Painted flowers were popular on Crazy Quilts for reasons given by a reader who wrote to the *Ohio Farmer* in 1884: "I painted flowers on some of the blocks. They are much prettier than embroidery and not so much work."

An unknown couple posed in a Rockford, Illinois photography studio about 1890. Her pose with fingers on a book, possibly signifying "the Good Book," may be meant to symbolize her piety. The fashionable crazy quilt on the table seems to add a contrasting note of worldliness. Collection of the author.

Elizabeth Waddle used a variety of textured silks such as velvet, brocade, chenille, satin and taffeta to make her Crazy Quilt, decorated with a few naturalistic florals. We recognize white lilacs, lily of the valley and a nosegay of rose buds. She may have drawn from life, but several pattern companies sold embroidery designs just like these, especially for Crazy Quilts.

<<< **Elizabeth Paulina Shinabarger Waddle**
United States, 1838-1913
Crazy Quilt with Sawtooth Border, circa
1880-1910
silk, cotton, acetate, piecing, embroidered
Gift of Mrs. Paul Roofe, 1982.0124
89 1/2" x 75"

This worn quilt from Sallie Casey Thayer's donation illustrates one of the goals of a teaching collection like that of the Spencer. Museums conserve objects for future generations. Many might view this stained quilt with its shattered fabrics as something not worth saving, but the design, in particular the quirky bowknot and swag border, offers inspiration to later generations. In the 1920s Rose Kretsinger seems to have been inspired by the border for her New Rose Tree quilt. In the twenty-first century Georganna Clark recreated the design as a small wall hanging.

<<< Georganna Clark
Lenexa, Kansas
Princess Feather, 2007
cotton, appliqué, quilting
25" x 25"

>>> Artist Unknown
United States
Princess Feather with Bowknot Border quilt,
circa 1840-1900
cotton, appliqué, quilting
William Bridges Thayer Memorial,
1928.0922
84" x 77 1/2"

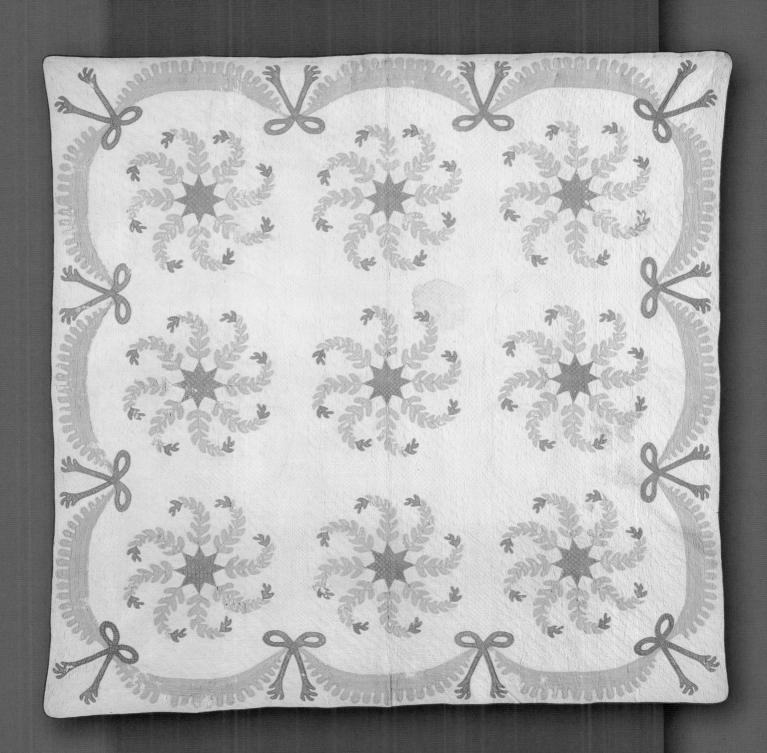

‹‹‹ Rose Frances Good Kretsinger
United States, Kansas, 1886-1963
New Rose Tree quilt, 1929
cotton, appliqué, quilting
Gift of Mary Kretsinger, Emporia, Kansas,
1971.0103
87" x 88"

Rose Kretsinger is considered one of the twentieth century's master quiltmakers. After she took up quiltmaking in the 1920s she traveled to Lawrence to study the old quilts at the University's Art Museum, believing new commercial trends produced quilts she called "tiresome." She may have borrowed her composition from the antique Princess Feather quilt, modifying the elements of bowknot and swag to more conventional proportions. Because the quilts here inspired Rose, her daughter donated the Kretsinger collection of 15 quilts to the museum.

*C*indy Korb's Emporia Rose is a sampler of patterns found in quilts made by Rose Kretsinger and her circle of friends in the years 1925-1950. The wreath in the alternate blocks was inspired by the central wreath in the New Rose Tree.

>>> **Cindy Korb**
Tonganoxie, Kansas
Emporia Rose, 2003
cotton, appliqué, quilting
87" x 87"

$\mathcal{I}$n the 1970s Virginia Randles was one of a group of artists in Athens, Ohio, who recognized the need to showcase textile arts based on the quilt's form. With Nancy Crow and Francoise Barnes she organized Quilt National, a juried exhibition for quilts designed to be viewed on a vertical plane—textiles generally called "art quilts" today.

For her Paperweight Series she drew from traditions in Italian glass. The millefiori or millefleur paperweight is a glass globe embedded with shapes and colors reflecting a "thousand flowers."

<<< Virginia Randles
United States, Ohio, 1912-1996
Millefleur quilt, 1989
from Paperweight Series II
cotton, piecing, appliqué, quilting
Gift of Dr. Leland P. Randles in memory of
his wife, Virginia, 1996.0134

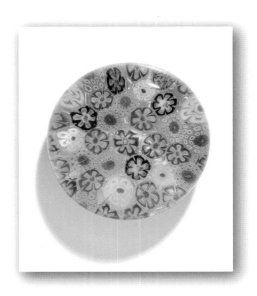

The Projects

In The Exhibit, you might have noticed photos of reproductions of quilts included in the Flora Botanica exhibit. Five projects, with instructions and patterns for making those quilts, are included in the pages that follow.

These instructions assume that stitchers have basic quilting and appliqué skills. There are many excellent Kansas City Star books that present that information, including *Hearts and Flowers: Hand Appliqué from Start to Finish* by Kathy Delaney.

FLOWER POT

Flower Pot by Doris Lux, Meriden, Kansas, 2007, 38 1/2" x 38 1/2".
Doris used a traditional color scheme for maximum graphic impact. She made some of her appliqué pieces three-dimensional by duplicating the pattern pieces, seaming two together face to face, turning them and attaching them only at one end. She added a wide binding to make a final frame. It shows 3/4" on the front of the quilt. See the original quilt on page 17.

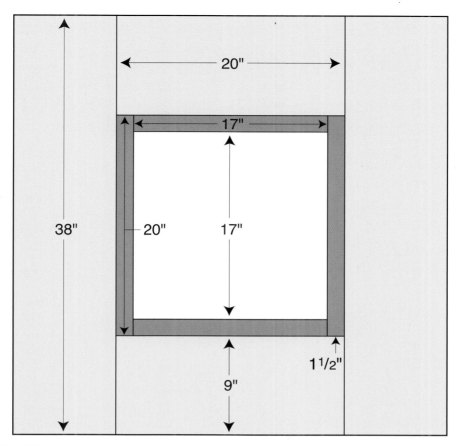

TO MAKE THIS 38" X 38" QUILT, YOU NEED:

- 1 center block finishing to 17"
- Inner border: 1 1/2"
- Outer border: 9"

FABRIC REQUIREMENTS

- 1 1/4 yards ivory for the appliqué background
- 1 yard red for the inner border, binding and appliqué
- 3 shades of green for the appliqué:
- 1 fat quarter of light green
- 1/2 yard of medium green
- 1 yard of dark green
- 1 fat quarter of yellow-gold for the appliqué

CUTTING THE APPLIQUÉ

- Cut a square larger than 17 1/2" x 17 1/2" for the center block's background. (When appliqué is complete, trim it to 17 1/2" x 17 1/2".)

- Cut strips of green bias finishing to 3/8" for the border vine and stems. You need about 8 yards.

- Refer to the templates for cutting instructions for the appliqué pieces. Add a scant 1/4" seam allowance to each pattern piece.

CUTTING THE BORDERS

INNER BORDER

- Cut 2" wide strips from the red:
- Cut 2 strips 17 1/2" for the top and bottom borders.
- Cut 2 strips 20 1/2" for the side borders.

BACKGROUND FOR OUTER BORDER

Cut 9 1/2" wide strips from the background fabric:
- Cut 2 strips 20 1/2" for the top and bottom borders.
- Cut 2 strips 38 1/2" for the side borders.

APPLIQUÉING THE CENTER BLOCK

- Fold the background square as shown and press to create placement lines.

- Prepare the appliqué pieces using your favorite method and place them on the background as indicated. Baste or glue in place.

- Appliqué, using your favorite method.

APPLIQUÉING THE BORDER

- Place the main bias vine in each of the borders (refer to the quilt photo on page 66) leaving extra length free at the ends for joining later.

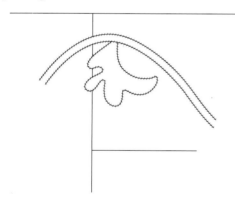

- Add the bias strip stems.

- Baste or glue in place.

- Prepare the leaves and flower parts using your favorite method and place them on the vine and stems. Baste or glue in place.

- Appliqué using your favorite method, leaving the ends of the bias vines loose for now.

SETTING THE QUILT

- Add the top and bottom red borders to the center block.

- Add the side red borders.

- Press.

- Add the top and bottom appliquéd borders.

- Add the appliquéd side borders.

- Join the vines by appliquéing the loose edges to curve around the corners.

QUILTING

- Doris echo quilted, following the shape of the appliqué designs, and added feathers to the sides of the border vine in selected spots.

BINDING

- Doris's wide binding provides a strong final frame for the quilt. To make it, cut single binding 2" wide. Place the binding on the top of the quilt with the edge 1/2" from the quilt edge. Stitch, using a 1/4" seam: the stitching line will be 3/4" in from the quilt edge. Turn and whipstitch the other turned under edge to the back side of the quilt.

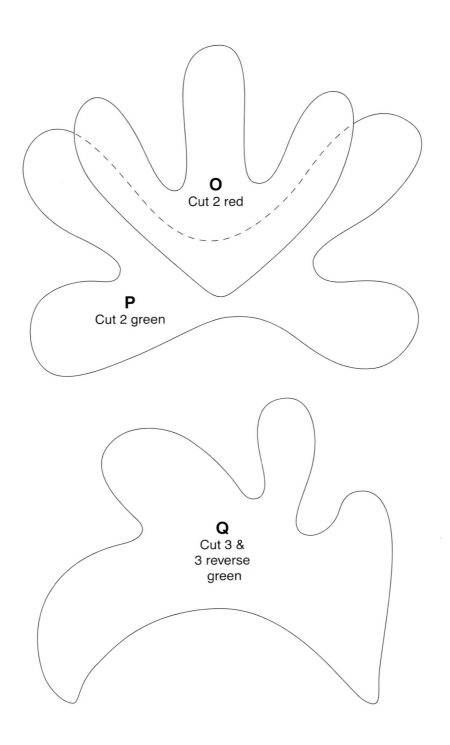

O
Cut 2 red

P
Cut 2 green

Q
Cut 3 &
3 reverse
green

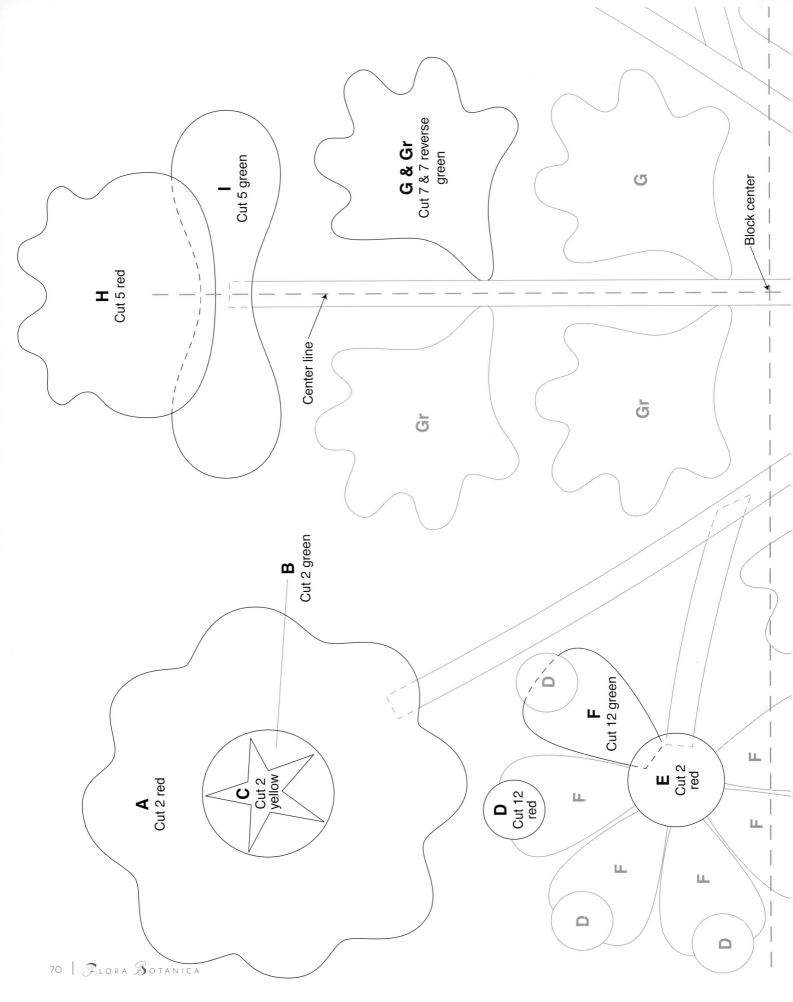

H
Cut 5 red

I
Cut 5 green

G & Gr
Cut 7 & 7 reverse
green

G

Gr

Gr

Block center

Center line

B
Cut 2 green

A
Cut 2 red

C
Cut 2
yellow

D
Cut 12
red

D

F
Cut 12 green

F

F

E
Cut 2
red

F

F

F

D

D

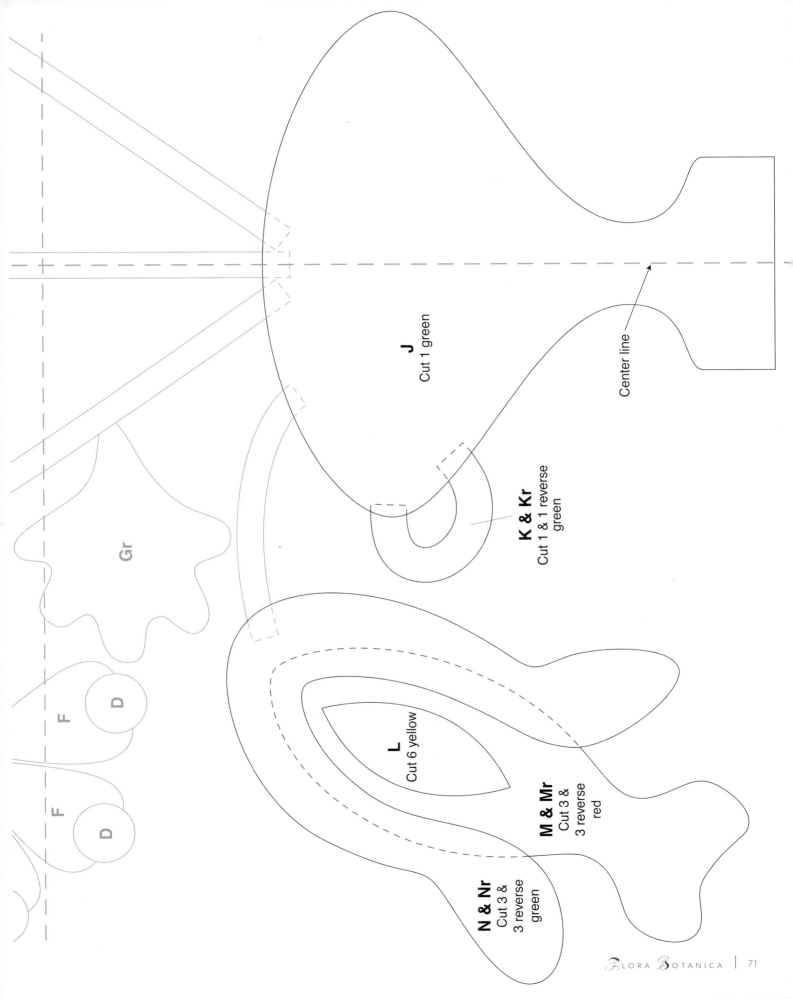

J
Cut 1 green

Center line

K & Kr
Cut 1 & 1 reverse
green

Gr

F
F

D
D

L
Cut 6 yellow

M & Mr
Cut 3 &
3 reverse
red

N & Nr
Cut 3 &
3 reverse
green

***Star and Crescent* by Julie McEathron, Lawrence, Kansas, 2007, 50" x 50".**
Julie created the quilt that might have been, a composition with intense colors before years
of use faded the fabrics. She pieced the blocks but you might prefer to appliqué the green
and red pieces to background squares 8 1/2" x 8 1/2". See the original quilt on page 25.

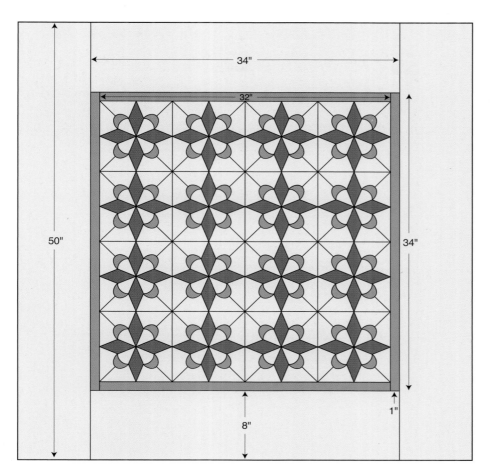

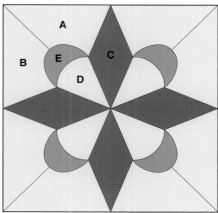

TO MAKE THIS 50" X 50" QUILT, YOU NEED:

- 16 blocks finishing to 8"
- Inner border finishing to 1"
- Outer appliquéd border finishing to 8"

FABRIC REQUIREMENTS

- 2 1/2 yards light for the background
- 1 1/2 yards green
- 1 yard red for inner border, patchwork and binding

CUTTING THE BLOCKS

- Cut your borders and bias stem before you cut the appliqué pieces.
- See the template pieces A-E for cutting instructions for each block.

CUTTING THE BORDERS

THE RED INNER BORDER

- Cut 2 strips 1 1/2" x 32 1/2" for the top and bottom borders.
- Cut 2 strips 1 1/2" x 34 1/2" for the side borders.
- The background for the appliquéd border
- Cut 2 strips 8 1/2" x 34 1/2" for the top and bottom borders.
- Cut 2 strips 8 1/2" x 50 1/2" for the side borders.

THE APPLIQUÉ

- Cut strips of green bias finishing to 3/8" for the vine in the border. You need about 8 yards.
- See the template pieces F-L for cutting instructions for the border appliqué.
- Note: all the leaves in the border are piece J.

PIECING THE BLOCKS

Piecing instructions follow. Refer to your favorite basic quilting instruction manual for the piecing techniques used in this block. You can find excellent instructions for curved piecing (page 4) and sewing set-in seams (page 68) in Kathy Delaney's *Beyond the Basics* (*Kansas City Star* books, 2007).

If you like to appliqué, this block could also be made by appliquéing the C and E pieces onto an 8" x 8" background.

- Sew A and B (reverse of A) together, creating a corner unit.

- Sew E to the D unit (creating a piece looking like an ice cream cone).

- Attach the D/E unit to the inside curve of the A/B unit.

- Repeat 4 times making 4 units.

- Attach C to the right side of each A/B/D/E unit.

- Sew together with set in seams (see advice above).

APPLIQUÉING THE BORDER

- Place the main bias vine in each of the borders as shown in the quilt photo on page 72, leaving extra length free at the ends for joining later.

- Baste or glue in place.

- Prepare the leaves, smaller stems and flower parts using your favorite method and place them on the vine (refer to the quilt photo for placement). Baste or glue in place.

- Appliqué using your favorite method, leaving the ends of the bias vines loose for now.

SETTING THE QUILT

Make 4 rows of 4 blocks each.

- Set these rows together to form the inner field.

- Add the top and bottom inner borders.

- Add the side inner borders.

- Add the top and bottom appliquéd borders.

- Add the side appliquéd borders.

- Join the bias vines at the corners.

QUILTING

Julie echo quilted the patchwork pieces by copying the shape of the appliqué. The original quiltmaker used a geometric grid in the diamonds and parallel diagonal lines through most of the background.

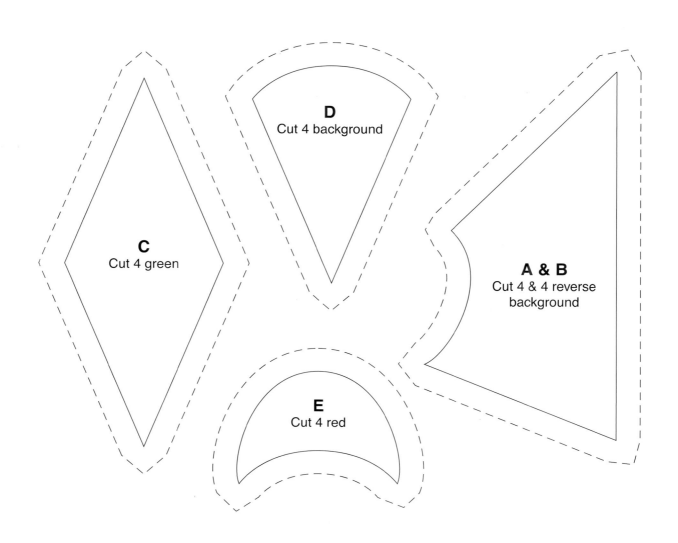

C
Cut 4 green

D
Cut 4 background

A & B
Cut 4 & 4 reverse
background

E
Cut 4 red

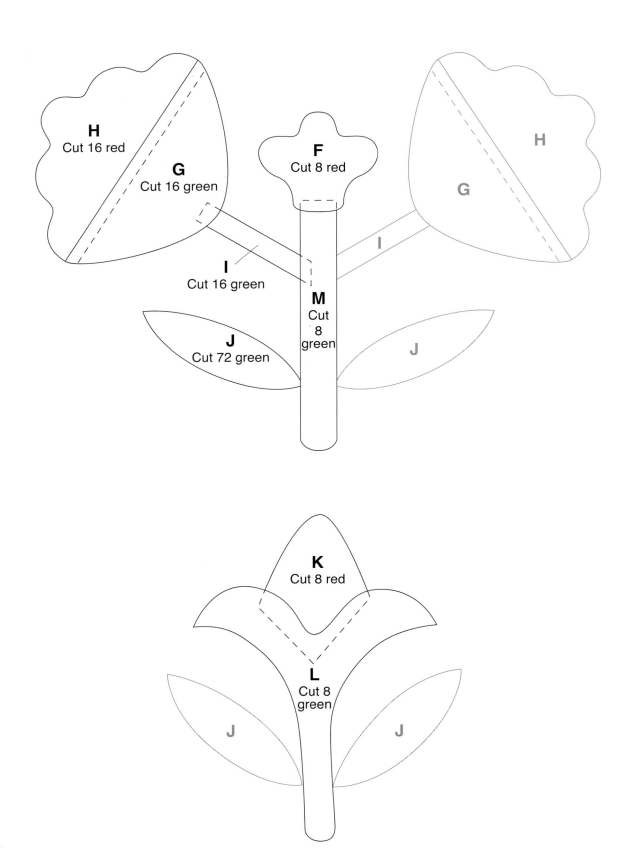

H
Cut 16 red

G
Cut 16 green

F
Cut 8 red

I
Cut 16 green

M
Cut
8
green

J
Cut 72 green

H

G

I

J

K
Cut 8 red

L
Cut 8
green

J

J

GOOSE TRACKS

Goose *Tracks* by Gail Stewart, Overland Park, Kansas, 2007, 40" x 40".
Gail created a close copy of the antique but added two borders for symmetry. She updated
the colors with a cooler yellow than the original chrome orange and used a tone-on-tone
ivory print for the background. Gail lives part of the year in Naples, Florida where this quilt
won a ribbon at the local guild show in 2007. See the original quilt on page 18.

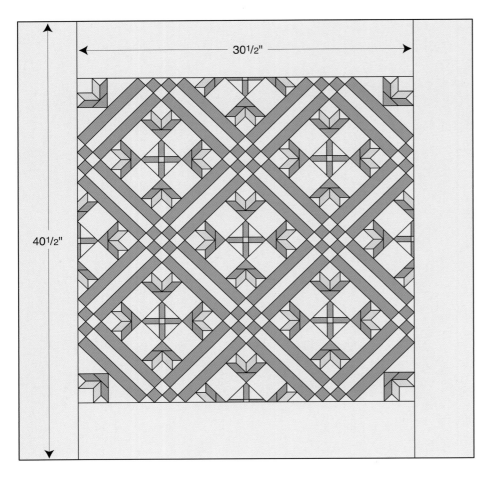

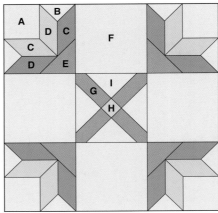

TO MAKE THE 40" X 40" QUILT, YOU NEED:

5 blocks finishing to 7 1/2"
4 half blocks
4 geese tracks for the corners
An appliquéd border finishing to 5"

FABRIC REQUIREMENTS

1 yard of green
1 yard of red
3/4 yard gold
2 yards of ivory white

CUTTING THE BLOCKS

For each of the 5 blocks:

🙠 A - Cut 4 squares of background fabric 1 7/8"
x 1 7/8"

🙠 B - Cut 2 squares of background fabric 2 1/4"
x 2 1/4". Cut each into 4 triangles with 2 cuts.
You need 8 triangles.

🙠 C/D - Use template C/D to cut the
parallelograms. Cut 4 green and 4 yellow for
piece C. Flip the template over and cut 4
green and 4 yellow for piece D. You may want
to mark piece D to differentiate the pieces.

🙠 E - Cut 2 red squares 2 1/4" x 2 1/4". Cut each
into 2 triangles. You need 4 triangles.

🙠 F - Cut 4 squares 3" x 3" of background
fabric.

🙠 G - Cut 4 red rectangles 1" x 2 1/4" and using
template G; trim the angles.

🙠 H - Cut 1 square 1" x 1" of background fabric.

🪶 I - Cut 1 square 3 1/8" of background fabric. Cut into 4 triangles with 2 cuts. You need 4 triangles.

CUTTING THE HALF BLOCKS FOR THE EDGE

For each of the 4 edge blocks:

🪶 A - Cut 1 square of background fabric 1 7/8" x 1 7/8"

🪶 B - Cut 1 square of background fabric 2 1/4" x 2 1/4". Cut into 4 triangles with 2 cuts. You need 4 triangles.

🪶 C/D - Use template C/D to cut the parallelograms. Cut 2 green and 2 yellow for piece C. Flip the template over and cut 2 green and 2 yellow for piece D. You may want to mark piece D to differentiate the pieces.

🪶 E - Cut 1 red square 2 1/4" x 2 1/4". Cut into 2 triangles. You need 1 triangle.

🪶 F - Cut 2 squares 3" x 3" of background fabric.

🪶 G - Cut 1 red rectangle 1" x 2 1/4" and using template G; trim the angles.

🪶 I - Cut 1 square 3 1/8" of background fabric. Cut into 4 triangles with 2 cuts. You need 2 triangles.

🪶 J - (half of G) Cut 2 red rectangles 3/4" x 2 1/4" and trim using template G (note there is a dotted line for J down the middle).

🪶 L – (half of H) Cut one rectangle 3/4" x 1".

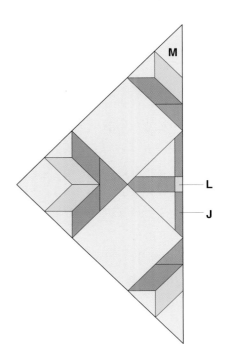

🪶 M - (half of A) Cut 1 square of background fabric 2 1/4" x 2 1/4". Cut into 2 triangles. You need 2 triangles.

CUTTING THE CORNER TRIANGLES WITH "GEESE TRACKS"

For all of the 4 corner triangles:

🪶 A - Cut 4 squares of background fabric 1 7/8" x 1 7/8"

🪶 B - Cut 2 squares of background fabric 2 1/4" x 2 1/4". Cut each into 4 triangles with 2 cuts. You need 8 triangles.

🪶 C/D - Use template C/D to cut the parallelograms. Cut 4 green and 4 yellow for piece C. Flip the template over and cut 4 green and 4 yellow for piece D. You may want to mark piece D to differentiate the pieces.

E - Cut 2 red squares 2 1/4" x 2 1/4". Cut each into 2 triangles. You need 4 triangles.

N - Cut 4 squares of background fabric 3 5/8". Cut each into 2 triangles. You need 8 triangles.

CUTTING THE SASHING

The pieced sashing finishes to 3" wide.

Cut the strips 1 1/2" wide x 8".

Cut 32 green strips.

Cut 16 white strips.

CUTTING THE CORNERSTONES

You need 4 nine-patches finishing to 3" for the cornerstones and 8 half nine-patch blocks for the sides.

O - Cut 32 green squares 1 1/2" x 1 1/2" and 28 white squares 1 1/2" x 1 1/2".

P - Cut 6 white squares 2 3/4" x 2 3/4". Cut each into 4 triangles with 2 cuts.

You need 24 triangles.

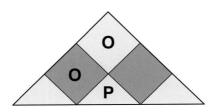

CUTTING THE BORDER BACKGROUND

Cut 5 1/2" strips from the background fabric.

Cut 2 strips 40 1/4" for the sides.

Cut 2 strips 30 1/4" for the top and bottom.

CUTTING THE APPLIQUÉ PIECES

Cut strips of green bias finishing to 3/8" for the border vine. You need about 8 yards.

Cut the flowers and leaves as directed on the templates, adding a scant 1/4" seam allowance.

PIECING THE BLOCKS

Create the corners—the geese tracks—by joining a green piece C and a yellow piece D.

Add a triangle B to create a C/D/B unit. Repeat to make 8 of these units following the color sequence in the illustration.

Join a pair of C/D/B units to create the tracks. Repeat 4 times.

Add square A to the corner. Repeat 4 times.

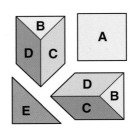

Add a triangle E to the base of the unit. Repeat 4 times.

Press.

Create the center square by beginning with the center diagonal, joining a rectangle G to either end of the square H.

Add a triangle I to either side of a rectangle G.

Repeat.

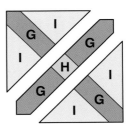

᠗ Join the diagonal units to create the center square.

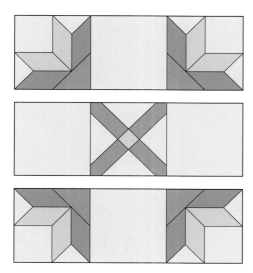

᠗ Add a square F to either side of the center square.

᠗ Seam a corner geese tracks unit to either side of square F. Repeat.

᠗ Join the 3 strips together, being careful to match the center seams.

APPLIQUÉING THE BORDER

᠗ Place the bias vine in each of the borders as shown in the quilt, leaving extra pieces free at the ends for joining later.

᠗ Baste or glue in place.

᠗ Insert the stems under the vine and baste or glue in place

᠗ Prepare the flowers and leaves using your favorite method and place them on the vine.

Leave parts of the flowers free at the tips to be stitched to the other border later.

᠗ Baste or glue in place.

᠗ Appliqué using your favorite method, leaving the ends of the bias vines loose for now.

SETTING THE QUILT

᠗ Piecing the sashing

᠗ Stitch 1 white and 2 green strips together to make striped sashing.

᠗ You need 16 sashing units.

᠗ Press.

᠗ Piecing the cornerstones

᠗ Alternate green and white squares O as shown to make nine-patches.

᠗ Make 4 nine-patch blocks.

᠗ Alternate 3 white triangles P with 2 green squares O and a white square O to make the edge triangles as shown.

᠗ You need 8 of these half-nine-patch triangles for the edges.

᠗ Press.

᠗ Piecing the corner triangles

᠗ Following the directions for the block corners create 4 corner squares.

᠗ Add a triangle N to either side as shown.

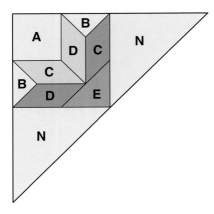

🕊 You need 4 geese tracks triangle units for the corners.

🕊 Press.

SETTING THE BLOCKS

🕊 Join blocks into 3 diagonal strips by alternating sashing with pieced blocks as shown in the diagram.

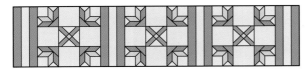

🕊 Create 4 sashing strips by alternating the striped sash with nine-patches and half nine-patches as shown.

🕊 Join the diagonal strips together, being careful to match the stripes and the nine-patch cornerstones.

🕊 Finish out the squares by adding the geese tracks triangle units to each corner.

BORDERS

🕊 Add the side borders.

🕊 Add the top and bottom borders.

🕊 Join the vines by appliquéing the loose edges to curve around the corners and finish appliquéing the tips of the flowers over the seams.

QUILTING

Gail Stewart hand quilted this in a very traditional manner. There are scrolls, flowers and leaves on the blocks. The border stitches echo the appliqué.

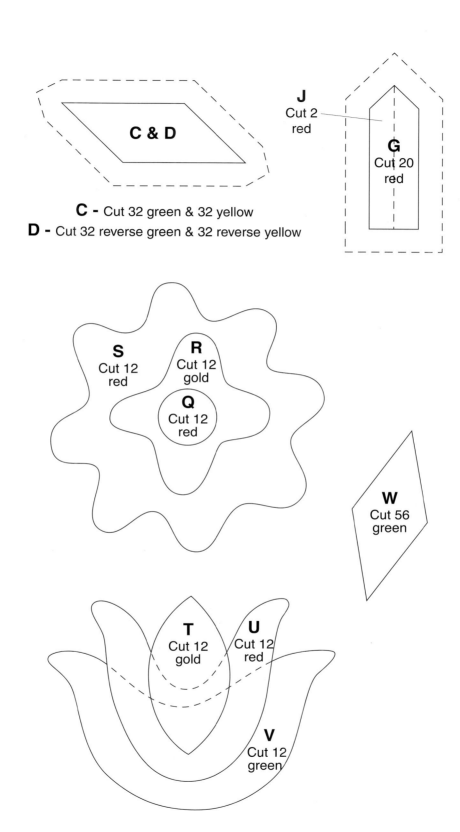

C & D

C - Cut 32 green & 32 yellow

D - Cut 32 reverse green & 32 reverse yellow

J
Cut 2
red

G
Cut 20
red

S
Cut 12
red

R
Cut 12
gold

Q
Cut 12
red

W
Cut 56
green

T
Cut 12
gold

U
Cut 12
red

V
Cut 12
green

DOVE IN THE WINDO

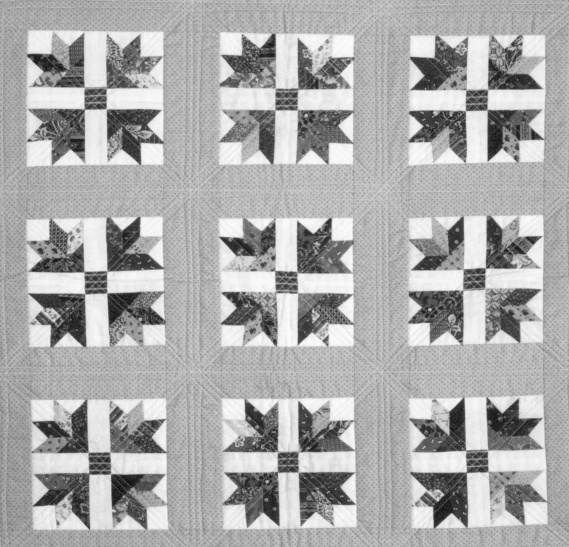

Dove in the Window **stitched by Jerrye Van Leer, quilted by Georgann**
Eglinski, Lawrence, Kansas, 2006, 28" x 28".
Jerrye loves to work in miniature, pulling from a big scrap bag of small reproduction prints.
See the original quilt on page 22.

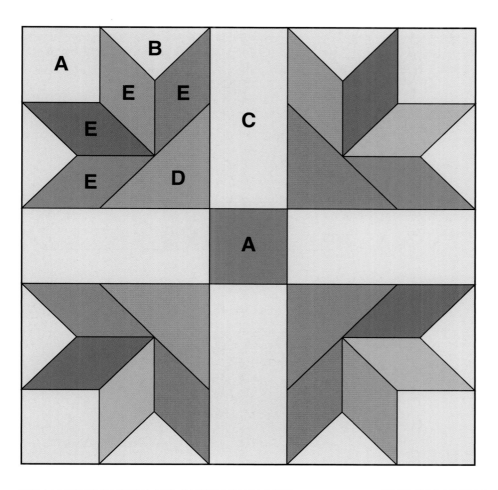

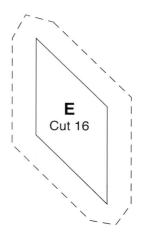

E
Cut 16

TO MAKE THE 28" X 28" QUILT, YOU NEED:

- 9 - 6" blocks
- 2 1/2" sashing and border

FABRIC REQUIREMENTS

- 1/2 yard of a double pink reproduction print for sashing and border
- 1/4 yard of green calico for the binding and center of each block
- 1/2 yard of light for the background (Jerrye used an ivory white to recreate the original.)

For the doves, Jerrye used a variety of reproduction prints. The diamonds and triangles could also be cut from 5" charm squares or 2 1/2" pre-cut strips (or buy 8 fat quarters of browns, pinks, blues and madder reds (brick reds)).

CUTTING THE BLOCKS

- A – Cut squares 1 1/2" x 1 1/2". Cut 4 light for background and 1 (green) print.

- B – Cut 2 squares of light background 2 3/4" x 2 3/4". Cut each into 4 triangles with 2 cuts. You need 8 triangles.

- C – Cut 4 rectangles of light background 1 1/2" x 3".

- D – Cut 2 squares of the same print 2 3/8". Cut each into 2 triangles. You need 4 triangles.

- E – Use the template to cut the E diamonds

from 4 different fabrics. Cut 1 1/4" strips of 2 print fabrics and cut 8 pieces, then cut 8 of 2 other fabrics.

CUTTING THE SASHING AND BORDER

- Cut strips 3" wide of the double pink reproduction.

- Cut 2 strips 28 1/2" long for the border sides.

- Cut 4 strips 23 1/2" long for the top and bottom borders and sashing strips.

- Cut 6 strips 6 1/2" long for the sashing between the blocks.

PIECING THE BLOCKS

- Piece pairs of diamond E together. Make 16 E/E units.

- Add triangle B to each pair. Make 16 B/E/E units.

- Create the doves by pairing 2 B/E/E units. Make 4 corner units.

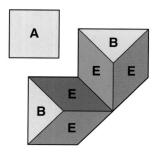

- Stitch a light square A into the corner of each corner unit.

- Add triangle D to the base of the corner unit to finish out the square. Repeat to make 4 squares.

- Piece a rectangle C to opposite sides of square A to create the central strip.

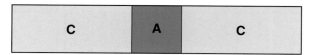

- Piece a corner unit to either side of a rectangle C. Repeat to create the top and bottom strips of the block.

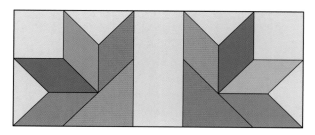

- Join the 3 strips, being careful to match the seams in the center square.

- Press.

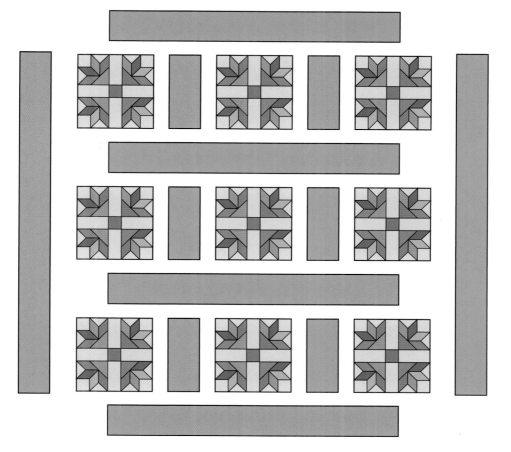

SETTING THE QUILT

- Make 3 strips by alternating a short sashing strip between the blocks.

- Stitch each of these strips to either side of the 23 1/2" sashing strips.

- Add the top and bottom borders, the remaining 23 1/2" strips.

- Finish by adding the longer side borders.

QUILTING

Georgann Eglinski machine quilted this by stitching three rows of diagonal lines through each block, extending into the sashing, which creates a wonderful diamond design. She added another three straight rows through the middle, the sashing and the borders.

SUGAR BOWL

Sugar Bowl by Gloria Donohue, Olathe, Kansas, 2007, 24 1/2" x 24 1/2".

See the original quilt on page 45.

The original basket quilt in green and red came with a note sewn to it that reads: "This quilt was pieced by Mrs. Margaret Cane in Delaware County, Ohio, in 1850. Quilted in Lawrence, Kansas, in 1867. After everything else was burned it was given to her daughter in 1883, Mrs. Lizzie C. Mann."

The 1880 census finds a Mrs. Elizabeth Mann living in Lawrence. She was born in Ohio about 1815. Mother Margaret Cane must have been born in the eighteenth century but she kept up with changing fashion. Her 1850 quilt was made in up-to-date colors and style, but she seems to have followed her own muse in her border design and the color placement in the basket handles. Gloria Donohue's copy retains the charm of the original with a softened color scheme.

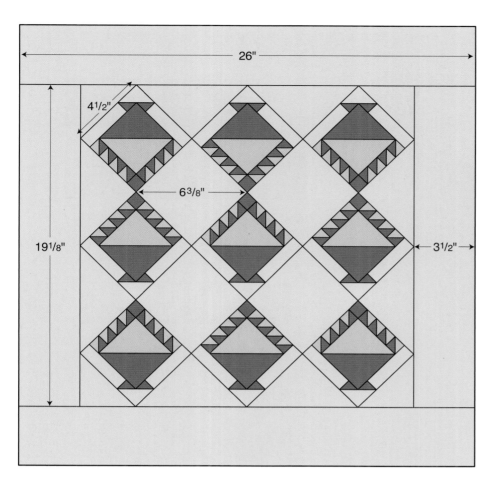

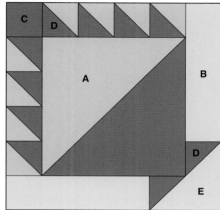

TO MAKE THE 24 1/2 X 24 1/2" QUILT, YOU NEED:

- 9 - 4 1/2" blocks
- 3 1/2" borders

FABRIC REQUIREMENTS

- 1 yard of ivory background (includes binding)
- 1/2 yard pink
- 1 yard green

CUTTING THE BLOCKS

- For each block cut the following. You need 9 blocks.

- A – Cut squares 3 7/8" x 3 7/8". Cut 1 green and 1 pink. Cut each into 2 triangles. You need 1 pink and 1 green triangle for each block.

- B – Cut 2 rectangles 1 1/4" x 3 1/2" of background fabric.

- C – Cut 1 square 1 1/4" of green fabric.

- D – Cut 1 5/8" squares: you need 4 pink and 5 green squares. Cut each into 2 triangles. You need 8 pink triangles and 10 green. Because these are so small, you may want to piece them as strips over a paper foundation. Use the paper piecing template (see page 90).

- E – Cut 1 square of background fabric 2 3/8" x 2 3/8". Cut into 2 triangles. You need 1 triangle for each block.

CUTTING THE SETTING PIECES OF BACKGROUND FABRIC

- Cut 4 squares 5" x 5".

- For the edge triangles cut 2 squares 7 5/8" x 7 5/8. Cut each into 4 triangles with 2 cuts. You need 8 triangles.

- For the corner triangles, cut 2 squares 4 1/8" x 4 1/8". Cut in half diagonally once. You need 4 triangles.

CUTTING THE BORDER BACKGROUNDS

- Cut 2 strips 4" x 19 5/8" for the side borders.

- Cut 2 white strips 4" x 26 5/8" for the top and bottom borders.

CUTTING THE APPLIQUÉ

- Cut the green leaves (appliqué pieces F and G) from the templates, adding a scant 1/4" seam allowance. You need 28 of each. Note that half of the G leaves are reversed.

- Cut strips of green bias finishing to 3/8" for the border vine. You need about 5 yards.

PIECING THE BLOCKS

- Piece a green and a pink triangle D together to make squares.

- Piece 4 of these D/D units into a strip. Make 2 of these strips. Usually we tell you to be careful in observing the direction of the seam line in these half-square blocks but Margaret Cane placed hers haphazardly and Gloria followed her example.

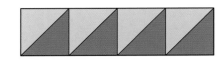

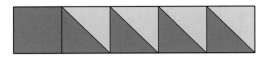

- Add square C to the end of one strip.

- Stitch a strip to either leg of the pink triangle A.

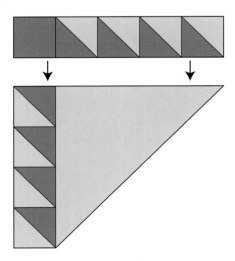

- Add a green triangle A to make a square.

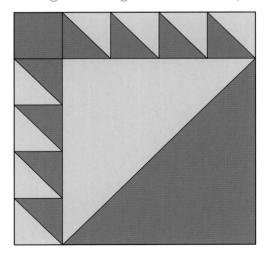

- Add a green triangle D to one end of rectangle B. Repeat going the opposite direction to make 2 mirror image B/D units.

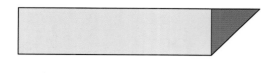

- 🐦 Piece a B/D unit to either side of the large square.
- 🐦 Finish out the square by adding triangle E to the corner.
- 🐦 Press.

APPLIQUÉING THE BORDER

- 🐦 Place the bias vine in each of the borders as shown in the quilt leaving extra pieces free at the ends for joining later.

- 🐦 Baste or glue in place.
- 🐦 Prepare the leaves using your favorite method and place them on the vine. Notice the informal way Gloria paired her leaves in imitation of Margaret Cane's original.
- 🐦 Baste or glue in place.
- 🐦 Appliqué using your favorite method, leaving the ends of the bias vines loose for now.

SETTING THE QUILT

Join blocks by creating diagonal strips as shown in the diagram. Alternate pieced blocks with setting squares and triangles. Gloria set one row upside down.

- 🐦 Add the side borders.
- 🐦 Add the top and bottom borders.
- 🐦 Join the vines by appliquéing the loose edges to curve around the corners.

QUILTING

Gloria used an old-fashioned design sometimes called elbow quilting, which echoes the block in concentric squares.

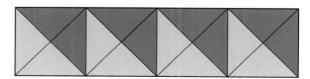

Paper piecing template

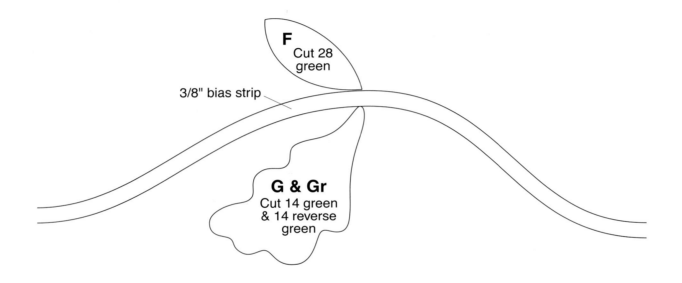

F
Cut 28
green

3/8" bias strip

G & Gr
Cut 14 green
& 14 reverse
green